Shiela,

I want to thank you so much for everything you've done for me! All the support and encouragement! Thanks too, for everything you do for the students of this district!

Blood Red Dawn

In praise of *Blood Red Dawn*...

"Mr. Shutt's words not only envoke in us a deep sense of awe for the bravery and the warrior ethos of the American Soldier, but a profound reverence for their heart, yearning for home and reaching out in compassion, even while in a state of constant fear and uncertainty."

—CJ Pride, Fellow Service Member

"Jon Shutt has literally gone from hell and back twice during his tours of duty in Iraq and Afghanistan, and he's now become a Virgil leading us straight down into a very real *Inferno*. He spares us nothing—from a desperate Afghan soldier amputating his own foot in the midst of battle to warm bread baked in a Kurdish oven as a gift to U.S. soldiers. The most powerful of these poems capture a tour of duty that kills and kills again the souls of those who survive yet show how one soldier's wounded heart still beats because of what continues to spring to life, even in the midst of war."

—Michael Trammell, editor of *Apalachee Review*

Blood Red Dawn

Jon Shutt

Kitsune Books
Quality books for eclectic readers

Blood Red Dawn

Copyright © Jon Shutt
May 31, 2012

All rights reserved. No part of this book may be reproduced in any form without the expressed written permission of the publisher, except by a reviewer.

Kitsune Books
P.O. Box 1154
Crawfordville, FL 32326-1154

www.kitsunebooks.com
contact@kitsunebooks.com

Printed in USA
First printing in 2012

ISBN-13: 978-0-9827409-9-6
Library of Congress Control Number: 2011944951

Front cover photo: Dan Gallagher

First edition

Disclaimer: All names included in this book are fictional and any semblance to another person's name is purely coincidental.

Acknowledgments

I would like to acknowledge U.S. service members, past and present, for their willingness to give the ultimate sacrifice for this great nation. Your courage and patriotism inspire me. May this stand as an everlasting thank you for your service.

Furthermore, I want to recognize those from 2nd Platoon, Cco 172nd INF (MTN), especially weapons squad—Thanks for watching my back and filling my days with laughter. A special thanks goes out to Arsenault, Boynton and Delbene—your camaraderie and friendship is a continuous, unspoken benefit of wearing the uniform.

*This book is dedicated to my family.
Thank you for your unyielding support and encouragement.*

Contents

Part I – Iraq: 2004-2005

Therapy *13*
Cast Iron Heart *14*
Rival Factions *15*
After the First Round... *16*
Muzzle *17*
He Is Going to Be a Hero *18*
Lessons in Kurdish *20*
Blood Red Dawn *22*
Peanut Butter *23*
Possibilities *24*
Squinting at the Sun *26*
This Empty Shell *27*
The Stench of Vodka *28*
It May as Well Have Been *30*
From the Hands of a Friend *31*
Here, Between the Tigris and Euphrates *32*
My Love and Iraq: Thieves of the Same Ilk *34*
Rewired *35*
The Allure of Murder *36*
A Small Miracle *37*
Soot Covered Hands and the Arsonist's Smile *39*
What They Won't Tell You and What They Will *41*
Friends and Family *43*
Intangible *44*
A Requiem for Sergeant First Class Jenson *46*

Part II – Afghanistan: 2010

Improvised Explosive Devices *51*
A Midnight Cacophony *52*
Metallic Angels *54*
The Worst Is Over *55*
Vamos a Bailar *57*
The Future *58*
T-Bone Steaks and a Bottle of JP8 *59*
With This Bullet *60*
The Promise of Spring *61*
The Distance *62*
In This Mag *64*
Simplicity *66*
Helpless *67*
Puppeteers *68*
A Truth Untold, a Lie Unchecked *69*
150 Meters and a Mile of Memories *70*
Freedom *72*
A Diamond Field of Smoldering Pasts *73*
An Uncle Undeterred *74*
The Timeline, the Deadline, and the Long Haul *75*
Swallowed *76*
Composition B *77*
The Mechanical Clown *78*
Swallows *80*
Laughing *81*
You Can't Kill Superman *82*
Waiting on Margaret *84*
A Longing for Vividness *86*
Playing War *87*
The Medic, the Wolves, and the Hero *88*
Tomorrow Never Comes *90*
The Crimson Shard *91*
The Scarlet Stain *92*
The Painter, the Wordsmith, and the False Advertisement *93*
Six-Times the Zoom, Ten-Times the Memory *95*

A Thousand Revenges *97*
Your Average Afghan Worker *98*
Life Through a Window Screen *99*
Outta the Shit *100*
Stuck *101*
Lullaby *102*
The Sands of Time *103*
Autumn's Offering *104*
A Faceless Provider *105*
The Art of the 21st Century *106*
Behind Smiling Eyes *107*
Toleration for the Mundane *108*

About Jon Shutt *109*

PART I

Iraq:

2004 – 2005

There is a wide world out there, my friend, full of pain,
but filled with joy as well. The former keeps you on the path
of growth, and the latter makes the journey tolerable.

— *Sojourn*, R. A. Salvatore

Therapy

They say I should seek therapy—
well here it is.

I'll put it down on paper myself
and skip the middle man.

I can formulate my own diagnosis—
PTSD.

I'll prescribe my own treatment—
Poetry.

I don't need a doctorate
to know this helps.

You want me to seek therapy?
Well, I'll pick up my pen and do just that.

Cast Iron Heart

I've built myself a new heart,
out of solder and cast iron.
And though it beats
with a metallic sound;
It keeps me from feeling.

I've replaced the valves
with iron shutters;
readying myself
for war,
and death,
and the depression
afterwards.

I've replaced the arteries
and the veins
with iron conduit.
Allowing my blood
to flow without feeling.

And it'll keep beating
and ringing my ears.
Pounding with
metallic resonance.

This is what it means
to be a soldier.
They've trained my mind
and sculpted my figure.
Then sent me to war
to harden.

Rival Factions

Equipped in full battle rattle, Ash and I
point our weapons out over the desert hillside.
Alert. Ready.

Goat herders sit around a fire,
their pack mules nearby grazing, their AKs
loaded. Ready.

Their herd grazes on sparse grass,
completely comfortable with the idea
of war.

The sun beats down on rival factions
unnerving, relentless, he chooses
no sides.

The moon, sitting next to the sun, doesn't understand
the concept of Sunnie or Shiite and only sees
senseless fighting.

The vultures battle the dunes
over the right to
fresh meat.

The wind moves dunes over
a bloody battlefield, leaving no traces of life
or death.

As day turns to night
the stars twinkle over
wasted lives.

After the First Round...

You don't seriously think about death
until after the first round explodes,
taking out a nearby fence. You sit paralyzed
as everyone else takes cover.

After the first round,
your perspective suddenly changes.
You're the first to take cover because you run
for it at the slightest rumble. This keeps you alive.

Your perspective suddenly changes.
You find yourself the first man cowering in a C-Barrier
at the slightest rumble because it keeps you alive
if mortars start falling.

You find yourself scouring your surroundings for C-Barriers
because you're never safe in the open
when mortars start falling.
Death stalks you from above.

You're never safe in the open,
even with kevlar and flack Jacket,
when death is stalking you from above.
You never escape this feeling.

Kevlars and flack jackets become permanent fixtures,
and this is how you begin to live,
because you can never escape
the sharp cracking explosions that haunt.

This is how you begin to live,
paralysis ebbing, you scramble for cover in your living room
from the sharp crack of haunting explosions.
You suddenly take death seriously.

(Muzzle)

Restless yet comfortable sleep created by a rifle's muzzle.
Though it poked and jabbed, it was reassuring to lie with that muzzle.

When we finally reached the top, the sky shone red.
Bright red, like the flash of a fired rifle's muzzle.

All those hopes pure and white,
tarnished black by carbon from the muzzle.

After the explosion that day, everyone was somber,
With two days before Christmas, it was our spirits they muzzled.

The hate built up until our vision was engulfed in red.
We bore our teeth ready to bite, wanting to bite, except our mouths had been muzzled.

He walked up slowly shaking his head, his face white
Carrying Frenchie's weapon by the muzzle.

I stood staring at pure beauty, thinking the sky had never looked so blue.
Everything stopped; only the wind was audible. Everything else was muzzled.

He Is Going to Be a Hero

Abdul Hafiz sits in his beat up Toyota wagon,
palms sweaty, excitement building with every breath.
Today he is going to make a difference.
Today he is going to strike the enemy a deadly blow.

He drives through the town of Diana
breathing deep the crisp, morning air.
Driving slowly in order to take in everything possible.
Every image. Every sound. Every feeling.

Driving slowly so as to avoid upsetting his load.

He goes through the market district,
watching Kurdish shop owners lifting their metal
garage doors in order to show their wares:
fruits, vegetables, trinkets and rugs—
the best in Iraq and the cheapest too.

He turns down a long drive,
a mountainside to the left of him
and a field of tall grass to his right,
slowly drawing closer.
Nothing stands in his way.

This is going to make him a hero.
The thought is comforting.
Then why is he so scared?
Why is his shirt soaked completely through?
And why is he shaking uncontrollably?

His vision blurs and his thoughts
drift back to his wife,
still sleeping in bed.
Her long, black hair
slinking its way across her pillow—
beautiful, peaceful.
She sleeps deeply,

spooning the vacant
half of the bed.

She has no idea of the hero
he is going to become.
He takes in a sharp breath
and realizes he hasn't been breathing.

His Toyota drifts across the road
and he yanks hard at the wheel without thinking.
His load shifts sharply with the sudden jerk.

There is no scream,
no moment of regret or ecstasy...
only the cacophonous blast—

The last thing his eyes see
before they are mercilessly seared
from their sockets,
is failure.
He is still 200 meters from his objective—
the gate to their base.

The neighborhood shakes
as shrapnel pounds the mountainside
and parts the tall grass of the field.
Abdul's wife jolts upright
a discordance ringing her ears.

Lessons in Kurdish

I took my lunch breaks sitting on the roof,
dangling my feet over the side,
waiting for Fatima.

She was usually nearby playing,
keeping an eye out
for me to appear.

She would greet me in Kurdish: "Joni Bashi!"
and I her in English: "Hi, how are you?"
Then we'd begin our lessons.

She'd begin counting
and I would repeat her.
Then we'd do it in English, roles reversed.

Yek, du, se
One, two, three
car, penc, ses

Each day would bring
more numbers or phrases,
whatever we could easily teach one another.

She never asked for anything,
though the boys she played with
begged for money and water.

She'd scare them away
or make them quit begging
and eagerly continue the lesson.

One of the last days I saw her,
she threw me up a small charm,
a token of friendship.

When I see that charm today,
hanging with my dog tags,
I am reminded of one young girl
who taught this soldier
a language of greeting.

Blood-Red Dawn

I'm going home—palms sweaty, anticipation choking me.
Excitement begins stirring
as I day dream about living normally:
she'll be there waiting; tears of joy falling
quietly down her cheeks. We can get back to our lives *together*.
I'll leave the jut and crack of gunfire and explosions behind,
and return to the surprise of teaching. Life can only get better;
after war, happiness should be easy to find.

How ignorant to have dreamed for normalcy. It's gone.
With tears blurring her vision she walked away and left me utterly alone.
The burst of gunfire haunts. Surely, happiness died back in the war-zone.
How can I fight depression when I awake every morning to a
blood-red dawn?
Everything has changed; I was foolish to think it would stay the same.
I'm craving something that never came.

Peanut Butter

The first one shook the building
with an ear splitting crack.
I nearly flew out of my cot
as I sat up straight, looking into the bleary
eyes of Mavis across from me.

Chaos broke out before the second even hit,
some meat-head outside was running
back and forth yelling,
"It's the real deal! Scrap metal everywhere!"
I'm sure he meant shrapnel. Dumb ass.

Immediately everyone begins arguing
about what we should do.
"Just stay inside and wait for orders.
This isn't the first time we've been attacked
by mortars you know!" SSG Stanton yelled.

Stratford stands in the middle of the room,
in full battle rattle, wild eyed and ready.
"Those weren't mortars," he screams,
"those were fucking rockets! We're being attacked
and instead of going out and getting those bastards,
you want us to cower in here and spread
Peanut butter on our assholes!"

The room is divided—
Those craving to defend
ourselves from terrorists
and those who understand
the spineless tactics of our enemies.

Exhausted, I put on my kevlar and my vest,
lie back on my cot,
and resume sleep.
Tomorrow's going to be a long day.

Possibilities

I watched as the star
came crashing down,
a glimmer of hope
over a sprawling,
wasteland.

Suddenly there were
a thousand options,
a thousand possibilities,
and they were all within
my desperate grasp.

I sat bouncing along
in the back of a Humvee,
my weapon pointed out
at the passing wasteland,
but it was all a blur.

The star—
came crashing down.

No time to think,
no time to ponder
consequences.
The possibilities
were too endless.

Only, time to act.

I spat it out—
I wish I were home!

The star burnt out
over the desert horizon.
I sat bouncing along
in the back of a Humvee,
shame slapping me in the face.

The star was long gone,
crashing over some other sky.
I was still here and the war
waged on around me,
but it was all a blur—

My mind was racing
through all the wasted possibilities.

Squinting at the Sun

I spoke with the Sun today
as he climbed up over
this war-torn oasis.

He mentioned your name
and as I squinted at him,
smiling at the thought of you,
he mentioned he saw you
halfway across the world.

He wasn't smiling.

He just beat down on me
with unrelenting heat
and I began to sweat.

Oh so softly
he spoke your name again,
but it was laced with malice
and encased in a subtle hint.
A warning.

And as I squinted
back up at him
tears rolled down my cheeks
and my eyes burnt.

I was no longer smiling.

This Empty Shell

Everything is gone...
Everything but this empty shell.
And the wind blows through
with a whistle and an echo—
Much like the deserts of Kuwait,
not a mirage in sight
to elicit even the tiniest bit of happiness.

The only thing the previous inhabitant
left behind, other than expended shells and shrapnel,
were these feelings of sorrow and agony—
that swallow up any possible new occupants.
Vultures circle high and flies buzz low.

The sign by the entrance reads:
"Welcome to my Heart"

The Stench of Vodka

On the floor,
drunk and babbling.
Weeping and spluttering,
I swung fists at the skeletons

that the vodka had helped
to drag out of my closet.
I lost myself in my recent past
and spilled my guts.

On the floor and wiping
snot off my face, you held me.
You held me—and I shook
with the tremors of my recent past.

And as you tried to console me
I think we both realized
I was in a fragile state.
I swear I didn't come here for this.

Drunk and yelling at my ghosts
in the bathroom mirror
I finally crumbled to the floor
in exhaustion.

How could I fight them
with my defenses down?
I swear the alcohol
made them stronger.

Screaming at ghosts in the mirror
I broke down—
and told you everything.
I poured it all out,

weeping and spluttering,
right there on your
bathroom floor.
I knew I couldn't save them—

yet, in a drunken stupor
with you watching
I tried like hell
and failed again.

Lost and ashamed
I balled my fists
all the tighter and
threw them at my ghosts.

How did the alcohol
make them so strong?
Weeping and spluttering
incoherent nonsense

I poured out my heart—
right there on your
bathroom floor.
I can never bring them back.

Lost and ashamed,
drunk and babbling,
crumbled in a heap and
wiping snot off my face,

I poured out my war stories
with the stench of cheap
vodka on my breath.
It wasn't why I came but

it happened none-the-less
and to be honest,
I can't blame you
for never calling me back.

It May as Well Have Been...

Sitting shotgun in a 5-ton
I hold onto a Nerf football a friend sent
to give to the local children.

They can run circles
around us with a soccer ball,
but can't throw or even
hold an American football.

I watch as we drive by Kurds
coming out from their religious services.
I look one young boy squarely
in the eyes and without saying a word,
throw the football right into his chest.

Catching the ball, he quickly
squeezes it tightly to himself
and sprints away, only looking back
to see if any of the other boys
are gaining on him.

I could have thrown him a grenade.

Whatever will he do with the football?
I don't know and I'm sure—
he doesn't either.
He just clutches the awkward thing,
a little jewel an American threw to him,
and sprints as fast as he can for home.

Other kids chase after him,
wanting whatever it is he holds.
It doesn't matter what it is.
An American threw it.

I may as well have thrown him gold.

From the Hands of a Friend

"Make up my mind!"
I yell while standing in the back of a green 5-ton truck.
Green—in the fucking desert.
Idiots.
"Go here," sergeant Stanton, my squad leader, yells at me.
"No there," sergeant Johnson, my platoon sergeant, directs me.
"Actually, they need an electrician at Diamondback,"
sergeant Laflour, 2nd squad's leader, reminds us all.
"But he's on this project, not the one at Diamondback!"
sergeant Stanton reminds him with a look that says,
"mind your own business." Which, he never does.
I have no say in this.
Hell, they wouldn't listen if I did.
I just climb out one green truck and into another and then back out again.
Three different trucks and I've been in each
more than once already this morning.
Communication is non-existent in this unit.
The leadership is just as communicatively incompetent
as they are color-blind.
Idiots.
The sun is beating down on us at 7 a.m. like its noon already.
I'm sweating my ass off and sick of hopping from truck to truck for
sergeants who can't seem to talk to each other before we start our day.
As I stand with arms in the air, aggravated as all Hell, Benton, the joker and
a good friend of mine, steps up beside the truck.
"Hey Shutt," he yells up at me. I look over to see him rubbing his eyes,
pretending to cry like a baby.
Everyone else begins laughing at his joke but I don't find it very funny.
Something inside me snaps.
 As he turns to walk away laughing, I let out all my pent up frustration.
With all my might I hurl my Kevlar at him.
Benton.
My friend.

Here, Between the Tigris and Euphrates

This place is Hell
and I'll tell you why.
Here souls are heard screaming, "Fire!"
Even in the dead of winter.

I'll tell you why.
The sand burns like fire,
even in the dead of winter,
as it whips across your face.

The sand burns like fire.
The children beg for water
as the sand whips around their feet.
Mr.! Mr.! Water! Water !

The children beg for water
with cracked, parched lips.
Mr.! Mr.! Water! Water !
They rasp. Their lungs on fire.

With cracked parched lips,
souls beg for Allah to free them.
Their pleading's hoarse. Their lungs on fire.
Kissing Hell's carpet, the souls beg.

Souls beg for Allah to free them.
There is no peace. There is no rest.
Lips touch fiery sand as the souls beg and beg.
AK spatter and mortar blasts are constant.

There is no peace. There is no rest.
It smells of death, decay and burning trash.
AK spatter and mortar blasts are constant
in this sprawling desert wasteland.

It smells of death, decay and burning trash.
Here, between the Tigris and Euphrates,
lies a sprawling desert wasteland
where life ends and ends and ends.

Here, between the Tigris and Euphrates,
demons herd souls through sandblasted fire.
Life just ends and ends and ends.

This place is Hell.

My Love and Iraq: Thieves of the Same Ilk
Demob., 2005

Autumn bleeds red on these open palms...
You took from me something I can never have again.
But that's what I wanted, right?
Still, you cried as autumn splattered across your palms.
You try to cleanse them in an open wound
that is my heart...
But autumn bleeds red on these open palms.

As my core grows cold as winter, the outside shivers, and with autumn
comes change...
But change is what I wanted, right?
Yet I fight as autumn splatters across my palms.
I try to cleanse them in an open wound
that is my heart...
But autumn bleeds red on these open palms.

In the heat and sand of the desert,
I longed to see a New England autumn,
so full of beauty and color.
But the landscape smears a haunting red
as autumn bleeds out into a cold, dead winter.
I try to stem the open wound.
But autumn bleeds red on these open palms.

Relentless—autumn bleeds red.

Rewired

A moment of hesitation,
I know what I'm supposed to do.

Run into her arms,
Kiss her face,
Caress her hair,
Do something!
Feel something!

An awkward moment of hesitation,
Who is she again?

Somewhere, in the recess of my mind
A chorus rings out:

Your heart's allowed
To feel something now.

Your heart's allowed
To feel something.

And though I know this—

I don't.

And I don't think I can
Ever again.

The neural connections
Between heart and brain
Have been disconnected
I'm sure I've been rewired

For my heart—is numb.

The Allure of Murder

Middle school students never hesitate
to ask the questions everyone's thinking.

*You were in Iraq. That means you've killed
somebody, right?*

Did you shoot anyone?

*Have you ever thrown a live
grenade at someone?*

*Are the terrorists all deformed
and weird looking?*

Did you slit anyone's throat?

Did you shoot anyone? Did you kill anyone?
Did you kill anyone? Did you kill!?

When the answers leave my lips,
for some reason—
I wish I were lying.

A Small Miracle

We sat Indian style
on the floor around
a large tablecloth
on the porch of a
small hut.

The family was hard
at work preparing a
feast for us in honor
of all we had done
for the village.

Which, to us,
was not much.
But to them—
it was like a
small miracle.

It was then that
I truly understood that,
electricity was something
I had taken for granted
before coming to Iraq.

This village had
never had a light
shining brightly
from a single window
in its entire existence.

In the span of an hour
we had laid down
a generator and a
distribution panel.
Soon they would have
more than lights.

The family placed
a stack of flat bread,
the best I've ever had,
in the middle of the
tablecloth, among bowls

of rice and plates
of chicken. It was a
basic Kurdish meal,
but it must have been
everything this one small,

struggling, family could
possibly muster up.
It wasn't anything extravagant
but it was the best meal
I had in my year in Iraq.

They had done all of this
to show their gratitude
to America and its soldiers.

It was my turn
to be grateful.

Soot Covered Hands and The Arsonist's Smile
—What It Is To Burn—

I'm burning every memory of you...
Every memory of us.

Watching as the flames lick at your face...
Turning your skin to ash.
Turning beauty to ash.
Finally, charred black flesh
to match your black heart.

Throwing these ashes to the wind...
Wishing for a better life,
without you.
Throwing your ashes to the wind.

For too long I let you hold my heart
in your clawed hands.
Now you're burning with it
for it was the catalyst of this
funeral fire.

I'm burning every memory of you...
Every memory of us.
Waving goodbye with soot covered hands...
Saying good riddance with an arsonists smile.

Watching in delight as
the flames devour your
horned halo.
Devouring everything I thought made me happy.
Devouring the lies.
Watching in delight, as the flames,
devour you.

Throwing these ashes to the wind...
Wishing for a better life,
without you.
Throwing your ashes to the wind.

Finally, you know what it is—to burn.
Finally, we have something in common.

And look darling...
The moon has come out in full tonight—
To witness your death
To witness the death of our love
To witness me spreading your ashes
next to the remains of the bridges—
we burnt so long ago.

I'm burning every memory of you.
Every memory of us.

Throwing these ashes to the wind.
Wishing for a better life,
without you.
Waving goodbye with soot covered hands...
Saying good riddance with an arsonists smile...

I'm burning these pictures
These pictures of us
Pictures of you
I'm burning these pictures...

Goodbye—Good Riddance

Throwing, your ashes to the wind...

And the Germans killed the Jews
And the Jews killed the Arabs
And the Arabs killed the hostages
And that is the news...

-Roger Waters-

What They Won't Tell You—and What They Will

They won't tell you about
the prisoners with heat and A/C
while many of our soldiers
sleep without a fan.

No. They'd rather plaster you with images
of naked bodies stacked high by soldiers
because cruelty is what shocks you.

They won't show you
smiles on Arabs' faces
for the jobs provided them.
For the freedom provided them.

They won't tell you
of the work done by engineers,
unless one of us dies doing it.
OH! Dead, they'll gladly give us the front page!

They won't show you
the happy, grateful smiles of the Kurds
as one by one lights across their village
beam brightly for the first time in years.

They won't show you
the schools we built
of solid concrete.
Utilizing a tarred and shingled

wood roof full of skylights
to allow plenty of natural light
during those ever present times
of fluctuating electricity.

They don't show you, because that is
simply—just not what you want to see.

You won't go talk with your friends
about the humanitarian effort.
But you'll spout on and on
about the death count.

You'll turn on your TV
morning after morning,
night after night,
to find it.

U.S. casualties:
3780—and counting.

They won't tell you about
any sort of happiness in Iraq
because statistics and ratings
say you don't want to hear it.

So instead they flash images
of death and destruction.
Battered buildings, and bleeding bodies.
Because that is what you're screaming for.

That's what you want to see.

Friends and Family

None of you knew.
You really never
needed to I guess.
It was all internal anyway—

At least I hope it was.
That is, I hope it never showed
on the outside just
how tore up I was inside.

The fact is, that if
it wasn't for you all
just being around,
smiling and laughing,

I'm not sure I would
have recovered with
so few scars.
It's true, I was a mess.

Depressed and confused,
I tried to find my place again
somewhere in the civilian life.
A little lamb, lost in the wild

streets of civilization.
Without a rifle, without orders;
Left to decide for myself—
What to do next.

None of you knew.
You really never
needed to I guess.
It was all internal anyway—

I just needed you there,
smiling and laughing.
Bringing light to the darkness
that was engulfing me.

Intangible

This is the poem
I've avoided writing
for so long.

This is the feeling,
the experience,
that's been so hard
to put down on paper.

It's just not tangible.

I know I wouldn't be the same
without it.
That year in the sandbox-

I know I can never get it back
and for years, that's all I wanted.
More than even the years to come,

I wanted
        that one year
                back.

                But now.
                Now,
           I wouldn't have it
               any other way.

               Call it change.
             Call it acceptance.

                  Iraq,
                the war,
                   and
             the aftermath

It's made me into
the man I am today.

And for that—I'm better.

Call it
Pride.

A Requiem for Sergeant First Class Jenson

Unlike the others, your death was silent.
There was no explosion,
no gunfire, no helicopters.
No calls for a med-evac.
Just the long steady beep
of the heart monitor
as you slipped into the afterlife
with Frenchie.

When you passed I
was in such a whirlwind
of excitement,
ready to get back
to my family and my life.
You easily slipped
from my thoughts.
As easily as the sun slipped
over that desert horizon
day after day.

I often forget you.
Avoid thinking about your death,
so soon after leading us
safely home.
When I *do* remember
I feel so guilty, so ashamed...
guilty for not grieving
like I did for Frenchie.

Caught up in
my own life,
I missed
your quiet departure.

Maybe that's why I
can never shake
the feeling of remorse.

Remorse, for having been
that empty chair
at your funeral.
For never letting you know
that I am grateful for all
that you did for me.

All that you did for us.

You never let
the war take your life,
and you did your best
to protect ours.
That is something
I'll never forget.

I let you go
without ever telling you this.

PART II

Afghanistan: Mar – Dec 2010

"The hardest part of coming home again
is when you realize you're not
the same person who left"

Justice League of America: The Lightning Saga, Brad Meltzer

Improvised Explosive Devices (IED's)

Let's start with the basics here boys,
You have several different types.
Complacency kills, so pay attention:

Victim Operated – that is, you drive over a pressure plate
Or through a trip wire—Kaboom!
Command Wire—Detonation Cord run out to a trigger man who triggers
the bitch as you drive by—Blam!
Radio Controlled—Even easier! Less wire to hide. Set the phone
to a certain freq. and punch it in—Sayounara!
Lastly, who can forget the VBIED's and Suicide Bombers—
one comes at you on foot and the other on wheels—
You're fucked either way, plain and simple.

Complacency Kills!
So listen up as to how you can counter IED's.
Take a look at these videos:

Humvee's blow to pieces...
Bodies fly—
"Believe it or not, that guy lived"
Shaky videos of real life incidents.

Lesson learned?
Squeeze those ass cheeks a bit tighter—
This is gonna suck!

That's your training for today men.
Good luck and God speed.

A Midnight Cacophony

                    The creak and groan of mattresses
                                            toss turn toss
    sleeping bag rustles
            Swish swash swish

                    Palm to flesh symphonies
Shish—Shish—Shish
                                Frantic individual ecstasy
            toss turn toss

                  Midnight outbursts
    "Somebody's fucking with me!"
                              mumbles and bumbles
             incoherence

creak spring creak
            sleeping bag rustles
                          palm to flesh symphonies
        mumbles and bumbles

                  Sporadic flatulence
    Tiny music—
            Tick, tick, tick
Beep—beep—beep—beep

                          Toss turn toss
    Thump, slam—stubbed toe
            Tap—Tap—Tap
                          Clang, bash "oops"

        click—clack
                chicken peck
finger tap

        toss turn toss
                Shish—Shish—Shish

A midnight
Cacophony

                        One man's insomnia
                        Becomes another's

                                        An arm outstretched
desperately groping
                    earplugs...
                                      Toss turn toss

Metallic Angels

Metallic angels
Suspended from heaven
On invisible strings
Soar overhead.

Propelled by cries
for assistance.
Raining down shards of lead
on these desert mongrels.

Their dance so divine.

Swift and deadly—
Falling, gliding, diving.
Soaring, climbing, recalculating
Descending again.

I want to play them a song,
Clap my hands and sing them praises.
Make Gods of these silver eagles
And profess my loyalty to their violence.

The sound of their guns—
a dirge. The sound of beauty
in the face of death.

The Worst Is Over

Take heart,
the hardest part is over.
From here on out
it's only "Hello's."

Take it day by day
and remember
I love you.

Telephone calls
and snail mail letters.
Facebook updates
and e-mail messages.

All to let you know
I'm alive and well
and missing you
every day.

Trust in me,
as I trust in you.
The hardest part is over.
From here on out
it's only "Hello's."

Telephone calls
and snail mail letters.
Facebook updates
and e-mail messages.

This pain is simply longing
and can't last forever.
Just wait and see—
The worst is over.

Our Goodbye's are done
and someday soon
I'll slip into your arms
and whisper, "Hello—

I'm back where I belong."

Vamos a Bailar

I had a dream last night
on the brink of awake.

You greeted me
at the door with a smile
and took my hand in yours.

Somewhere in the distance
The Gipsy Kings played

Vamos a Bailar.

And so, with the music in our ears,
love in our hearts,
and happiness sparkling in our eyes—

We danced
And laughed
And sang
And danced

And danced

And danced.

All the while,
the cats played
at our feet.

The Future

"My wife and I are going to have kids!"

"I'm gonna buy a piece of land and
build my own house."

"I'm saving up my money to buy a new
Corolla so I can give my old one to my girl."

"I'm going into the porn business!
No man, seriously. You think I'm
fucking around—but I'm serious. Porn."

The future.

Old and young we all
discuss it with fervor.
Eyes sparkle bright and
faces light up with excitement.

It could be all we have.
It could be lost on the tail wind
of and RPG round.

The future.

Soldiers hold onto it with
Incredible strength,
Despite the fact
that for us,
It is so
amazingly
fragile.

T-Bone Steaks and a Bottle of JP8

JP8, that's what started the charcoal.
Pre-burnt chunks of wood
Blazing bright till the diesel burnt off
Then turning to coal.
Grill's ready.

There is something about a grill
That just screams America!
T-bone steaks and burgers,
Grilled to order.
Inhale America.

The sun smiled
down on us all.
The same one that smiled
Down on our loved ones yesterday.
I grilled my heart out.

Everyone lined up,
Plates in hand, ready for
A piece of America.

The Afghan mountains
Stood tall around us
We could pretend it was
New Hampshire.

There is something about a grill
That just screams America!

The smell of steaks
Rolled through the air
Covering the usual
Stench of feces and burnt trash
That is Afghanistan.

Just a dab of JP8
And this desert mountainside
Will blaze—America.

With This Bullet

With this bullet—
I could shatter lives.

I could take my own.

Brains splattered behind
my crumbling corpse.

The stock is collapsible
just like my life.
Muzzle in mouth.
Trigger within reach.

8 pounds of pressure's
all that's needed.
Little silver pin
drives forward.

Powder explodes.
Lead glides through
rifled steel.
Leaving in its wake
wisps of carbon,

spatters of gray matter,
and my crumbling corpse.
Empty soul—hollow eyes

Shades of brown, hazel,
green, blue, gray

loll back to see
green rolling pastures
azure skies

peace?

The Promise of Spring

Everyday withers by,
falling away like a
blackened, wilted pedal
of a rose at war
with autumn.

The fragrance of beauty
begins to dissipate –
Replaced by the stench
of decay and looming death.

Daily, the rose
battles on—
The promise of spring
driving it ever onward.

Onward, until the day
when the last pedal
clings to its stem
in desperation.

Dreading its fall
yet knowing it's inescapable.
Mother Nature must
run its course.

In the face of a
waning autumn,
the pedal blackens completely
before letting go...

This isn't death
but rather,
the promise of
Life.

The Distance

Black
Pitch black
No sight of the hand
Held in front of him.

Click.
Green.
A green illumination
And the hand appears
Blurry—as the lens
Is focused for distance.

And the distance holds
A rough terrain,
Encased in mountains
Climbing like Jack's stalk
Towards the heavens.

Yet it is not the distance
That holds his attention
At least not as much as the
Next 50 meters.

The green halo
Spies a wadi in the
Soft clay.
Shit!

Not another one.
Not another creek of
Shit water.

Sopping wet he stands
On the brink
Of decisiveness.

Left, Right, Left—
Soldiers are
Jumping
Slopping
Wading
Swimming.

Decision made—
A few strides backwards,
A quick sprint forwards
Spring!
Airborne...

Weapon raised,
Legs spread wide
The gap closes
As his body sinks and

SLAM!
Too short.

His chest crashes
Into the far ledge
And his face slams
Into soft clay.

Blink.
Green shimmers and fades
The black engulfs everything
As does the water.
Shit!

In This Mag

In this mag there are 30 ways to say—
$\qquad\qquad\qquad\qquad$ I hate you.

Each with its own green tip
Dripping with the disease
You bring upon your nation.

30 ways to make you pay for your lethargy, for your gluttony,
$\qquad\qquad\qquad\qquad\qquad\qquad\qquad$ for robbing us blind.

take
$\qquad$ take
$\qquad\qquad$ take

These bullets are all I have left to give—So come, get your fill.

In this mag there are 30 ways to say—
$\qquad\qquad\qquad\qquad$ You disgust me.

Each with its own brass shell
Which your survivors
Will surely pilfer.

30 ways to spit out the foul taste
$\qquad\qquad\qquad$ you leave in my heart.

30 ways to show my loath for the way you
$\qquad\qquad\qquad\qquad$ prey upon our kindness.

For the way you
$\qquad$ refuse to save yourselves.

You crave pity.

You disgust me.

This mag has 30 blasts to drown out
$\qquad\qquad\qquad\qquad$ the din of your excuses.

Your country will never rise.
        You will continue to rot because you fail
                to cut the limb above the gangrene.

    I only pray
        that with your death
            I'll rid myself of the foul taste that plagues my heart.

Simplicity

It's simple.
It's just because.

Just because
you are what I look
forward to,
day in, day out.

Just because
I know you'll
wait for me
patient and loyal.

Just because
the way your smile
lights up your face
makes me fall in love
all over again.

It's simple.
It's just because.

Just because
it's your love that helps me
open my eyes...to another
Afghan morning.

Helpless

Again, I'm left behind to
sit in the truck—Helpless.
While war wages on
in the distance.

I know all those guys
out there and all I do
is sit here helpless,
listening to broken radio traffic—

"I copy four KIA.... Schhhheeeee—Squelch.
Roger, one WIA... Whhheeeep—Urgent."

My heart pounds at the
speed of sound—
BOOM.
Meanwhile, the truck just idles.

I should be out there with them.

Explosions and gunshots
rattle my brain from within a
stationary vehicle. Yet it's only the
thought of not being out there that hurts.

All I can do is sit here,
imprisoned and immobile,
while the battle continues.

Helicopters fly low overhead
as the sun goes down in a
dazzling display of colors.
I feel helpless

trying to decipher this broken radio traffic.
Scheeeee—Wheeep—Squelch
Urgent.

Puppeteers

The Artist leaned back in his chair and smiled—
He could see it now, his newest creation would soon
Entertain millions.
He picked up the strings and with the flick of his wrist
The puppet danced and danced—it obeyed his every command.
He could see millions smiling and laughing at his creation.

Years later, a warlord taught these puppets to hold a rifle—
He could see it now, his newest creation would soon
Destroy millions.
He picked up the strings and with the flick of his wrist
The puppet squeezed the trigger—it obeyed his every command.
He could see millions crumbling and writhing in agony.

The warlord leaned back in his throne and smiled—
Thus, war was created
and the artist wept.

A Truth Untold, a Lie Unchecked

I'm sorry for leaving you in the dark.
For making you think I'm still stuck
on base. For not letting you know that
I have been going out on missions.

But the truth is, it's better this way.
Better for you to think I was safe here
on base and not out there with the rest
of the guys. I'm sorry.

I don't think you'd understand though.
Understand how trapped I felt. How
stressful it was for me to be here feeling like
everyone's life rested in the palm of my hand.

Believe it or not, it's easier for me to be out
on missions, looking out for only my teammates
instead of a whole base. I can relax now.
I know it sounds strange, but you can't imagine

the weight that has been lifted off of my shoulders.

My only regret is that I can't tell you,
Or at least I can't bring myself to—
I'm sorry for leaving you in the dark.
Honestly, it's better this way.

150 Meters and a Mile of Memories

150 meters,
not so far to run
even in full kit.
You'd think it would be quick.

Yet it felt like hours
with the explosion on
repeat in the mind.
He'd never seen bodies fly so far.

Move feet, move!
How many times could
the image possibly replay
before he reached them?

He'd never seen bodies fly so far.
Whose were they?
Malforse and his men were up there.
Forty feet—straight up!

150 meters
felt like miles
the explosion—
body parts flying.

Whose were they?
It's amazing how quickly
the Afghan terrain can
take your breath away.

150 meters
and breathless.
Where's Malforse?
No U.S. casualties!

"Hey Mueller, you ever
High-five a dead man?"
Whose hand is that?
No U.S. casualties.

It was only the detainees.
One forty feet—straight up.
The other, in pieces.
A sigh of relief—even a smile.

Stepped on a landmine.
No U.S. casualties.
Only the detainees.
Talk about irony.

He'd never seen bodies fly so far.

Freedom

It can take a deployment
To help you see
The beauty in the little things.

Like picking the clothes
You'll wear for the day.
Or deciding where you'll spend the night.

It's these little freedoms
That we often crave.
The freedom of choice—
The choice to choose—freedom.

It can take a deployment
To make the things we took
For granted seem bittersweet.

To make the things
We took for granted
Everything!

It's funny, we fight for freedom
Yet to do so, we freely
Give our own.

A Diamond Field of Smoldering Pasts

Charred remains
of nothing in particular,
just clumps of soldiers' has beens really.
Freshly dumped and still smoldering.

Our waste—
Their ashen
diamond field
ripe for mining.

The nearby families
gather up their shovels
and wheel-barrels—
quick to make haste

to the pile
of steaming debris.
Ripe for mining.
What could today's ashes hold?

Sifting through waste.
Charred remains
of our useless,
smoldering, pasts.

Afghanistan,
the land of beggars,
thieves and scroungers.
The land of sand.

The land, of recycled pasts.

An Uncle Undeterred

They named you Hunter
and knowing your father,
I'm sure you'll live up
to the name.

I missed your birth
and will surely miss
the first six months
of your life.

But an Uncle cannot
be deterred and you can
rest assured that you'll
see plenty of me.

Your aunt says,
you have my feet,
square little bricks
with pebbles for toes.

How you got them,
I'm not sure. Regardless,
it makes me smile
and pity you at the same time.

Your pictures adorn
the plywood walls
of the closet I call
my room.

I smile when I see them
and think of the day
I'll finally get to meet
my little nephew.

They named you Hunter,
a nice strong name
that I am sure you will
easily live up to.

The Timeline, the Deadline and the Long Haul

18 months to begin
to pull out of this
God forsaken country.
Yet, I see no end in sight.

18 months and counting down
yet they keep expanding
bases, pouring foundations,
and paving airstrips.

18 months to pull out
and they just keep
pouring more in.
A last ditch effort?

One last hoo-rah?

ANA is incompetent
and beyond corrupt—
To say the least...
Good luck.

I can see no end
Nor any sign of a pull out.
18 months—
Yet, they keep pouring in.

Despite the deadline
being in plain view,
the timeline continues.

Swallowed

The chopper swung a hard left
and the countryside panned out in front of me.
An ocean of bleak sand—
spotted with impudence.

Specked with impertinent life,
green and beautiful.
It's beauty intensified by the desolation
that relentlessly tried to consume it.

Deep in my gut a fire burned,
I so desperately wanted that ocean
to open up and swallow the place whole.
All of it. All the beauty and life,
leaving behind nothing but a crater.

It is so much easier to hate
an ugly, desolate, lifeless land.
I didn't want a single thing in that country
to spark in me, any sense of compassion or humanity.

I'd rather swallow everything whole
and cough up the ashes.
Let them spill from my mouth,
a river of desolation.

Swallow it all and
leave nothing behind.
Nothing but the ashes
hanging from the corners of my mouth.

It would have been easier that way.
It would have made everything, that much easier.

Composition B

A small steel sphere,
2.5 inches in diameter,
sits perched on my chest
packed with 6.5 ounces
of composition B.

It's olive drab,
smooth and cool
to the touch and
it packs a punch—

5 meter killing radius
15 meter casualty radius
yet a single piece of shrapnel
can fly as far as 230 meters.

The M67 Fragmentation Grenade,
an anti-personnel explosive.
Weighing in at 14 ounces
it packs a punch.

14 ounces of
olive drab steel
sits aloft on my chest
in its own little pouch.

6.5 ounces of composition B.
So smooth, and cool to the touch.

I wonder,
how many years
has it waited,
for its chance
to detonate?

The Mechanical Clown

After smoothing over
the last load of gravel
I sat idling. Waiting,
for security to pull in

and mount up.
The crowd started to
grow around me.
Children and teenagers alike.

They stood wild eyed
and awestruck.
Gathered round the machine
like it was some sort of
circus act.

He pointed at the bucket
and made motions
of lifting and dumping,
so I obliged.

Up
Down
Lift
Dump

A mechanical clown
in a desert circus.
Entertaining the masses.

Up
Down
Lift
Dump

Children clapped and
laughed, jumping up and down.
Excitedly, waiting for the
next act to start...

Zormat is not a place where
sincere smiles come freely—

The mechanical clown felt obliged.

Swallows

Thump, Thump, Thump
Little black swallows,
Wings slicked back
In a straight dive,

Soaring over allies' heads.
Soaring over fields of sand.
Soaring, straight over incoming rounds.

To land with a deafening crack,
a bright flash and a fist-full of shrapnel.

Those thumps and the
Following explosions
A welcomed sound to
the ears of our comrades.

The trucks had arrived!
The big guns had arrived!
The MK-19 was there!

And all could tell.
Thump, Thump, Thump
Little black swallows of death—
Diving down upon their enemies!

Raining down destruction in
Three to five round bursts.
Thump, Thump, Thump.

Wings pulled back tight,
Beaks stretched straight out,
Soaring fast overhead—

The kamikaze dive of the swallow
A welcomed sight in deed.

Laughing

Looking around I see that they're all safe—
and no doubt, smiling.
We can laugh now, because we're all here.

Leaving the gunfire behind, waning in the wake
of artillery rounds, we can surly smile.
Amped up and screaming, everyone is reveling in the thrill of life.

In the thrill of having cheated death—again.

Another close call but,
                we can laugh now, because—we're all here.
We're all safe.

You Can't Kill Superman

The thought of death
Is usually easy to shake.
You shrug it off and laugh.
I mean, you can't kill Superman.

You've beaten the odds before,
That means you should easily
Be able to beat them again, right?
And thus, you shake the thought—of death.

But what do you do when you can't?
When it suddenly consumes you.
Odds stacked against you aren't so easy to beat.
At least, not this time.

Besides, Kryptonite is truly
An ass kicker!

You can see the casket,
Draped with the red
And white stripes—
A dark blue field of stars

One for each death you cheated.

Suddenly your suffocated and the lid won't open,
Nailed shut by each image of death that you've conjured up.
The thought has consumed you.
Crept in unexpectedly and left you watching your own funeral.

Damn it! You can't kill Superman!

You try and shake it off.
But the reaper hides in the dark recesses of your mind
Mocking, laughing, lurking.
How many more can you cheat?

So much life left to live,
But the casket lid slams down
With a resounding thud—
A draped flag...

        Red

                White

                        A blue field of stars.

Waiting on Margaret

Helicopters land daily,
floating down like
metallic grasshoppers caught
in a fresh summer breeze.

Soldiers around the FOB
can hear them landing
and they perk up with
renewed excitement.

Could this chopper
be bringing Margaret?

Yet, when the grasshopper
springs again to catch
another breeze heading
for some other base

and there is no sign of Margaret,
shoulders sag and heads bow.
A heavy gloom settles down again.
The bitch has abandoned us.

For most, Margaret is all
there is to look forward to.
Missions come and go.
Days wither on and on and on.

The war continues around us.

But the truth is—
we're just waiting on Margaret
and it's been weeks and still!
There has been no sign.

Most don't talk about it,
superstitiously believing that
to speak the name will
only delay it further.

Yet, you can sometimes hear
whisperings among the enlisted
as to when we'll see her again.
We're all just waiting on Margaret.
It's true that mail is the number one
morale booster for soldiers.

Missions go by and
the war continues.
We can handle that—
but it's tough waiting on Margaret.

A Longing for Vividness

The grasshopper sprung again,
catching a southerly breeze.
This time though, I sat in its belly
feeling the vibrations of its wings
as it drifted towards Sharana.

An eventual drift towards home...
and oh how I longed to be there
breathing in her scent once more.
Feeling her soft hair run through my fingers.
A deep longing ran through me.

A longing for the vividness
of her being, once more.
A vividness for the depth of her eyes.
Almond in color and ever changing in hue,
slightly changing in hue.

A testament—
for her ability to adapt.
I want that vividness back!
I want the vividness of her skin,
so soft to the touch.

The vividness of her smile,
dimpled and beautiful.
Encased in the softest,
fullest lips. Easily,
the centerpiece of her essence.

Oh, how I want
that vividness of her back.
It's sad how five months can
blur the edges of memory.
A snapshot from an unfocused camera.

Oh grasshopper, take me home.

Playing War

The truth is: I felt like a kid,
only, the weapon in my hand,
wasn't a stick and death is real.
Still, the little oasis of woods

was like childhood nostalgia
on the edge of Afghanistan.
We moved with ease for once.
Truly at home amongst the trees.

We blended in with their foliage,
kneeled at their bases,
used them as cover and concealment.
Yes, we were truly at home within their canopy.

Their lush greenness was a slap in the face.
The copse itself an image of defiance
to the harsh land around us.
The smell of leaves pounded our senses—

with nostalgia.

The truth is: I felt like a kid
playing war with friends.
But the weapon in my hand
wasn't grandeur of an over-imaginative mind.

It was real—and so was death.

The Medic, the Wolves, and the Hero

They ignored his calls.
His desperate calls for them
To wake up!
The calls that the enemy was there.

They ignored him as if he
Had once cried wolf.
And they paid for it.
He paid for it.

The enemy hit hard and they hit fast
And he was the only one to respond.
Grabbing a weapon and returning fire.
There was a sudden blast

As an RPG ripped through the air
Slicing it in a display of hatred.
It hit near the sole defender
And shredded his foot.

As it hung by a slick piece of skin
And a stubborn chunk of bone
The man pulled out a knife
And finished the job.

After deftly applying a tourniquet
And fighting off wave after wave
of nausea. He dragged himself back
To his weapon and continued to fight off

Wave after wave of enemy.
Bullets sliced the air and RPG's
Rocked the walls of the base
In a relentless barrage of anger.

When it was all said and done
And the man with his foot in hand
Stumbled back to those who had failed him,
Having had to defend the base alone

he said not a word
Out of spite or ire.
Only, "Help"...

And they laid him on a stretcher.
He was a hero.
He was an Afghan.

Tomorrow Never Comes

I'll stay awake all night
and pray that tomorrow
never comes.

Hide here in your arms
and hope the daylight
doesn't find me.

Tomorrow brings goodbyes.
Just the thought of them
tightens my chest.

I just wish the world would stop
and re-orbit itself
around our embrace.

The sun be damned.
We can find ourselves in the dark
with the radiance from our love.

Because there is nothing,
nothing more important
than this.

Nothing more important
than you and me.

Smile and tell me
you love me.
Tell me it'll be okay.

I'll stay awake all night
and hope that tomorrow
never comes.

Hide here in your arms
and pray the daylight
doesn't find me.

The Crimson Shard

From my bottom lip
I pluck a crystalline shard,
tiny—yet, gruesome.

Ruby red in hue
with dark crimson,
jagged edges.

My left ear pounds
as I roll this diminutive shard
between my fingers.

One little jagged, crimson shard
among the thousands
that speckle my face.

A haunting explosion—

I cringe as thousands
of minute shards
assault me.

A Scarlet Stain

As the glass shards whipped through the air,
driven by the explosion, the afternoon sun met their brilliance
and sent myriad colors dazzling over their target.
Basking him in radiance which, much as their hue,
would soon turn the brightest of reds.

A flash of crimson strewn across a stark white face,
amid a torrent of chaos. Scarlet rivulets ran as freely as the target did,
seeking refuge in the nearest fabric. A sudden desire to abandon the chaos;
To merely be absorbed into a peaceful, scarlet stain.

The Painter, The Wordsmith, and the False Advertisement

Paint yourself
in the saddest picture possible.
Poor and stumbling—
Suppressed and regressing.

Better yet,
have someone do it for you.
One who's better
with brush or words.

I still feel no pity.

I've stood on the edge of your desert,
shrouded by mountains,
letting the sun blister my skin.

I've watched your idleness
and felt first-hand
your corruption.

I've plagued myself with thoughts of rescue
without realizing that a country
which stands behind a flag
that means nothing to them
is beyond rescue.

Let the world cry out
against the wrongs delivered upon you.

I feel no pity.

For I've watched you deliver
those wrongs upon yourself.
Basking in your corruption.

You are the country that cried wolf.
Lying in a deceptive fetal position—
corruption blistering your heart.

I feel no pity.

A flag stirs with the wind,
rippling black, green and red.

Hide behind it—
for it means nothing to you.

The wind might as well
pick up—
and tear it to shreds.

Six-Times the Zoom, Ten-Times the Memory

An optic with a six-times zoom
can really clarify a situation—
can bring an enemy
clearly into focus.

A .50 caliber bullet is something
most people won't put themselves
in front of.

Packed with 671 grains
of gunpowder,
it can travel up to
3000 feet a second.

So it was in perfect clarity
and with superior firepower
that the gunner spied
the runt of a man
bringing an AK to bear.

A burst of gunfire rings out
loud, angry, superior.
Heavy recoils follow
but the optic stays crystal clear.

Ten to Twelve rounds
tear through flesh, bone and sinew
with unabated vengeance.

A pink mist erupts
before a gingered sunset.
Showering the horizon.

Eyes bulge
and the body rocks back
from the impact.

A limb falls useless
along with the AK
before the body crumples in agony.
Crumbles, behind a crimson haze.

An optic with a six-times zoom
can really clarify a situation—
creating a memory
that can be hard to erase.

A Thousand Revenges

One mortar—
sent emotions ablaze.
The flame reaching
an impeccable height.

One explosion—
resonated across the base
for over an hour.

For some it would resonate
for much, much longer.

One shattered window—
stood as a grim reminder
of how quickly everything
could fall apart.

One weapon—
sprayed
a thousand
revenges.

One life—
sat alone behind the wheel
on the brink of perceived safety.

The glass blew in
and somehow the shrapnel
parted around him, granting him—

one more chance.

Your Average Afghan Worker

You are the carpenters
arriving at the jobsite
without nails.

You are the writer
without pen or paper.

The cook without a stove.

Yet, you expect pay
to sit around drinking chi.

Take a look around your country
and realize
why it lies asunder—

It's because you are
merely the bacteria
in the world's largest Petri-dish.

Growing rapidly in your
slothful idleness—
feeding off the system.

Life Through a Window Screen

You've been living your life
Through a screened in window,
Seeing the world in waffled distortion.
Breathing in air through a piece of cloth.

Trapped in a costume,
Wandering like a ghost
Dressed in sheets.
Tell me your happy—

I'll read through the lie.
Tell me you do it for religious reasons...
I'll bite my tongue and
Choke on the taste of iron.

Tell me, does Mohammad so cloister
All his followers? Or only those he sees
As less than significant?
You allow your men to enslave you.

Go ahead and lie to me—tell me you're happy.

When was the last time:
You breathed in crisp air unfiltered?
You saw your deserts and mountains in clarity?
When was the last time,

You saw life—Unveiled?

Outta the Shit

"Give me the beat boys to free my soul
I wanna get lost in your Rock 'n' roll
And drift away."

The lyrics and ensuing melody crept through our headsets
as we crept over the rugged terrain.
Just as we've crept through this deployment.

I gripped the steering wheel and sung along
Trying to keep the MRAP from lurching,
Rocking, bumping and shaking its way down the dusty road.

Just a mounted patrol, easy enough.
Yet, Greyson's words echoed in the back of my mind
Interrupting the melody—

"I'd say, 'We're outta the shit now'
but this is Afghanistan.
That never really happens."

He couldn't have made a truer statement.

For months we've blistered under this sun
Choked on the swirling, spiraling dust
And dreamed of home.

Dreamed of being "Outta the Shit".

The melody crept back in—

"Give me the beat boys to free my soul
I wanna get lost in your Rock 'n' roll
And drift away."

Stuck

Years of searching
and I finally found
the needle in the haystack.
And when I did, she stuck me
and I bled—true love.

Lullaby

Sing me a lullaby.
Even if it's the last thing I hear,

The mortar can tear through the sky
And speckle this body
With gruesome, metallic pox.
I'll just melt into a crimson stain on the field.

As long as you sing me a lullaby

I can easily let the bullet pierce this heart
And collapse these lungs.
I'll crumple in a shower of gunpowder
And let the next breeze carry me towards
The sound of your voice

Singing me to sleep.

Eternity rests on those lips—
Waiting to catch the wind
And flutter into a lullaby.

I really couldn't ask for anything more.

The Sands of Time

The wind picks up into another sandstorm.
The distant mountains
and everything between
are lost in a sandy haze.

An ember glows bright red and
a cigar burns down a little lower.

The sands of time whip across the base,
weathering everything in its path.
The landscape, the buildings, Afghans, soldiers—
life in general. The sands, weather it all.

Ash hangs precariously to an apex.
Death—Holding on desperately
to the life burning beneath it.

As the wind shifts and gusts heavily,
the apex crumbles, scattering ashes to the wind.
Scattering, death to the wind.
This land deteriorates everything in it.

My cigar burns down to nothing.
The wind and sand snuffing out its life.

Autumn's Offering

Even here, miles away from New England,
I can feel her touch—deep down inside,
stirring memories with a tinge of nostalgia.
These plains and dusty mountains look remarkably
the same, though I feel the splatters of colors across my mind.

I feel the change that envelopes Autumn in a death grip
and just like her, I don't squirm or fight it, but revel in its beauty instead.
My senses reel in a newfound sensitivity that only she can stir
and each sense picks up another faded, weathered memory
from some old dusty attic that's held it gently aloft for years and
years and years.

The smell of crisp air on a wayward breeze and
I'm seventeen again and paddling a canoe across
a choppy lake with my brother, risking the chill winds
in nothing but a T-shirt and jeans. Slinging line across white caps
in hopes of the next big catch. Even if the only catch—is a cold.

A hard cold wind blows across my neck, raising goosebumps and
I'm fourteen again and in love, staying out late to kiss in the dark.
Hands roaming over soft skin, goose-bumped like my own.
Lips quiver and my body shudders with a shiver, as much from the wind—
as my own soaring lust; a late night Romeo on his way to his first
broken heart.

An oil drum, welded and crafted into a poor man's woodstove, sits
ingesting slivers of an old pallet and casting off a fiery glow to heat these
home-sick hearts.
The smell of it brings me back to you, back to where I want to be.
Cuddled on the couch by the woodstove, holding you close as the TV basks
us in a tranquil glow and Alex gives us another clue to answer in the form
of a question.

Though miles upon miles separate me from New England
and these dusty mountains cage me in a land of dreary shades of brown,
vivid, nostalgic, colors splatter across my mind—
an offering from Autumn.

A Faceless Provider

I love how you worked your way in
for the short sale.
A lover's gamble wherein you
consistently hold the winning hand.

Tell me, do you even
remember his name?
It's written right there
on the checks you cash!

He goes to war for his country,
risks his life daily,
and all you can do is
pocket his checks...

Do you even remember his embrace?
Or has it left you
the same way your loyalty did?
In a lustful fit of adultery.

Another soldier returning home
with only the lint in his pockets...
Another faceless provider, clutching a losing hand
while trying to put his life back together.

The Art of the 21ˢᵗ Century

Respect their culture.
Tolerate ignorance—
Empty your pockets for their sake.

Tell me:
Is shitting in a field considered culture?

IED's must be an art and therefore cultured...
Surely, playing for both teams is sportsman-like—
Sports are a part of culture that must be respected.

Tolerate ignorance—
Pour out green backs in a humanitarian effort.

"The remains of 6 soldiers killed by rogue Afghan cop come home"
Surely, playing for both teams is sportsman-like—
While our hands are bound by a thread of ROE.

Win their hearts and minds. Pity the Afghan people.
Pay your taxes—empty your pockets.

Give to those who have nothing...
nothing, but hatred and discontent for the hand that feeds.
Nothing but HME and traitorous thoughts
for those who pay their taxes—emptying their pockets.

Respect their culture.
Tolerate religion.
Protect their Mosques from possible retaliation...

One Somali-American Muslim plots to destroy thousands of Americans
and we scramble to protect the rest of the Muslims from "possible
retribution"...

Shitting on the side of the road is culture,
as cultured as the left hand that wiped the ass that shat.
And *that* we must respect.

Home-made explosives are the art of the 21ˢᵗ century.

Behind Smiling Eyes

You didn't go there alone—
Why would come back that way?

I don't care what the movies say—
No *one* man can win a war.

That includes the one during the aftermath.
The silent war raging behind smiling eyes.

Memories are broken movie reels
Skipping through faded images on mute.

And erasers are empty bottles
that smudge more than erase.

Faded images tear easily.
Much like the fabrics of sanity and emotion.

Sleepwalking through deserts and mountain ranges
Loosens one's grip,

but you can only fall as far as you've climbed.

We didn't go there alone—
We can sleepwalk together, behind smiling eyes.

No *one* man wins a war.

Toleration for the Mundane

The days tumble off the calendar
Drifting slowly to the floor...
Some—are easier than others;
While the others, are painfully drab.

The adventurer returned home,
forced to tolerate the mundane
amid a flourish of changes.

Changes in one's self,
One's surroundings, friends,
family, loved ones and work.

Time doesn't stop when you're not around.
And though it was never expected to,
It didn't need to move at such a drastic speed.
I mean, how does one make up so much lost ground?

You don't really...
You can't pick up where you left off—
And the pieces don't fit back together that easily anyway.
You leave that ground behind and blindly step ahead.

It's not easy.

People like to ask, "What was the hardest part?"
While it can be hard to admit
and it often surprises many
The truth of it is,

The hardest part is—coming back.

About Jon Shutt

Jon Shutt has served ten years in the Army National Guard as an Engineer. In 2004, he deployed with a Maine Engineer unit as an electrician where he spent most of his days doing construction projects around northern Iraq. In 2007 Jon earned his Bachelors degree in English Teaching from the University of New Hampshire and began teaching 5th grade in Lebanon, Maine in 2008. In late 2009 Jon put his teaching career on hold to deploy with a New Hampshire Infantry unit to Afghanistan. In Afghanistan he was primarily an assistant 240 gunner, but his Engineering skills kept him busy building tables, lofts, TV stands and other creature comforts in his off time.

Upon returning from Afghanistan in late 2010, Jon found his love for building propelling him into teaching woodshop to young, eager minds and hands, which is what he does today in Berwick, Maine. He and his wife, Monique, live in Milton Mills, New Hampshire.

CPSIA information can be obtained at www.ICGtesting.com
Printed in the USA
BVOW072305130512

289924BV00001B/7/P

9 780982 740996